POISONED HONEY, BITTER BLISS

TAPASYA MURALI

Foreword

Preface

1
Unwanted Flutter
The Distance Within
You, Who I Can Never Have
La Cuna

2
Sweet Killing Heart
The Last One

3
Let Me Go
Forgettance
My Love
Contradiction
Drought Of The Soul

4
Unspoken Devotion
The Weight Of Love
Living Death
Eternal Dance
Serendipity In The Void
Do You Doubt Me, My Love?
In The Labyrinth Of Time
Eternity In Your Embrace

5

Liminal
Echoes In The Storm
The Weight Of Unbelonging
The Silent Gaze

Foreword

"Poisoned honey, bitter bliss" is a collection of the poems I've written throughout my journey so far. They have been divided into sections of themes that I think fit them best, although I maybe mistaken myself. My poems differ on the way you interpret them, there is no right or wrong interpretation. Not all of these are based on my experience or point of view, some, more like a lot of these have been written to resonate with the reader rather than myself.

Also, quick disclaimer, none of these poems are connected to each other, this is merely a collection of the poems I've written, most of which are random thoughts and ideas I get during quite unconventional times and have written down in my notes app.

Preface

Hi, I'm Tapasya, you know? the one that wrote this book? Yeah, so I never had any idea whatsoever about publishing a book. When I was younger, I would write fanfiction stories and what really sparked my interest in poetry was my 6th grade writing assignment. We were given an assignment to learn and write different types of poems of which we could pick our own themes, I had picked life, which led to do a deep dive into the meaning of life, how to create poetry and such. This instantly struck a bell in my brain, leading me to put more effort than I even have into this one assignment. Later on, I developed a need to read, read anything and everything that had even a slight underlying meaning to it. I thought nothing of it at the time, but thinking back, these are the memories I recall that shaped my path for writing.

I started writing poetry in 9th grade (or so I remember). After showing it to my parents they brought up an idea of publishing a book, I didn't take it seriously. But as I began to grow, with both age and skills, many peers, friends, family, etc., that read the things I wrote suggested the same. So on one faithful day (that's today, 27/03/25), I decided to give it a shot, which is what I'm doing right now, well it would be in past tense whilst you're reading but you get the idea.

1

UNREQUITED

Unwanted Flutter

No, I'm not in love,

it's just a phase that'll fly above.

No, I'm not in love,

and I'll never be enough.

But then, why? Why,

do I get butterflies

whenever I see that pretty smile

spread over your face like a mini Nile?

How do I get all flustered,

when all I heard

was your name? It's absurd.

This feeling, it leaves me bewildered.

The Distance Within

The closer I get, the farther you are.

No matter how I try, I can't seem to abide

by these rules that hold me tight.

These contradictions, they hang loose

but the feelings that I use

just get me a new bruise.

A shining glimmer atop my head

is a curse that's fed

through the miseries of my fellow men.

You, who I can never have

In every part of me, there is you.

You lie eternally whilst I bask in your lighting presence.

Alas, your gaze longs for someone,

Someone who I will never be.

Those palms in no circumstances shall meet mine;

cursed and impure, tainted with sins and recline.

But when your eyes do meet mine, they show no exception,

glistening with the same fiery passion as when they meet another's.

Oh, how this flutter's my insides.

This feeling shan't be more, I plea.

For if it is, it'll ne're flea;

rotting my brain to insanity,

rendering me to nothing more than a filthy
dog.

Everything comes to a standstill

It's only me and a part of you that walk this
path of dread.

La Cuna

Each passing day,

you're drifting farther and farther away.

I'm afraid that one day

you'll leave me astray.

You let the wind sway you,

leaving me hanging on the willow tree.

But now, you are no more than a fading
memory.

2

LOVE'S TOXIC BLOOM

Sweet killing heart

A long silence is held

I look into your eyes

while you frantically gaze through mine.

The hues of umber and deep crimson

creep into the corners of my sight.

Looking at what you did,

it was a bloody mess

but that's what made me fall.

And I fell harder for you as time went on.

You brought to life my wildest dreams

no matter how corrupt or clean.

Each sight of every night,

then laying resting in your arms in a plight.

Once I lay thinking,

an idle mind with a full heart,

how much more could you do?

Then everything stops.

The eerie silence creeps in once again

but this time, I'm the bloody mess.

While you stand there, deepening your gaze,

I fell harder for you than I have any other day

You fulfilled my burning desire,

a question I longingly pondered.

And now, the delivered experience from your
own hands

I feel at bliss, even at my end.

You've finally showed me

what I have been hallucinating

my body in an abyss and my heart in paradise

I'll thank you once more, in the depths of hell
and

I can say, one faithful, bright sunny day

is when you'll appear to be at bay.

The Last One

My breathing; catching and heavy.

Vision blurred and disassociating,

hands; shaking and unresponsive.

Ears ringing; sensitive to the slightest noises.

Thoughts get clouded with one,

and only one need; the pellets.

I stumble over to the counter,

twitching fingers grab the bottle.

An uncontrolled rush surges through me,

fumbling over to open the lid.

I swallow; peace washes over me,

but in the end, only for a moment alone.

My head ripped out from underwater.

The haze clears; or so I believe.

Bliss flows through my veins,

beats in my chest become louder;

too loud. Suddenly, a pang hits me,

again and again and again.

I collapse, unconscious or dead,

something I'll never know.

3

ACHING ECHOES

Let me go

My life has ended, it's time for me to go.

But you've shackled me to this world,

with chains made of polyurethane tubes

and needles through my skin.

I've made peace with the fact that I'm gone;
have you not?

For long I've suffered,

spent my time curing instead to enjoying.

Now in these last moments,

I regret that mistake intensely(deeply)

I just wish to be free,

move on to my afterlife

or my next, should fate decide.

But for that, my dear, you need to let me go.

Accept that I am gone.

For it is no sad event;

celebrate as though I am still alive.

You would have freed me from suffering,

and that is enough to be glad.

You would have done me good,

that is, if you let me go.

So, let me go darling,

And celebrate my death instead.

Forgettance

Death is no great feat for me.

I keep wishing upon it every tomorrow.

For what is there left to be alive?

I've never been embraced into hands so warm
they melt me.

Nor have I done great deeds to keep me.

I don't fear death, never will I.

Living is a fear I have, but to be lived for is a
thought that shall continue to rot my brain.

In the end, it was neither death or living that I
feared; but being forgotten.

So, these words shall remain a testament for
my existence, though I'll never suffice,

maybe, just maybe these letters will survive.

My Love

You have been bestowed with the voice of the
angels,

yet you only utter the words of the devil.

How is it so that you can be both, my fallen
angel?

If looks could kill,

then you'd be a dagger; stabbing my heart out.

You leave me to bleed, cut me, hang me but

every time I am revived, I come back to you.

It's as though I live for you,

I was made for you.

And you are a punishment created for me, my
suffering.

Beautiful but deadly,

dainty but sharp,

simple yet threatening.

You loom over me;

I am on my knees;

control me and break me,

just to piece me back together.

When will this vicious cycle end?

I do not know nor do I anticipate it.

I will go through this torture;

look forward for more,

anticipating every move as long as it's you,

my love. My reason to re-live,

to be reborn, to cherish you and

embrace you with open arms

in every life, my darling death,

no matter the times you meet me.

Contradiction

Even though I find it hard to show,

being face with death,

I find myself afraid;

what of the things I've never done?

what of the people I've never met?

what of the love I've haven't experienced?

what of the touch I've never received?

The memories yet to be made, and the words
yet to be said.

Will I be the only sorrow within myself in a

world filled with elaborate tapestries of lies?

Shall the minds situated with mine be at peace
once I am gone?

Shall they remember me as a burden that has
been lifted?

Will my, finally dissipated, presence free their
spirits that are shackled to my body?

Am I afraid of the looming death that will

signify freedom for the people around me,

or of the insignificance of my life that serves

just the purpose of burdens others?

Drought of the Soul

A loved one's death,

a time of sorrow and grief,

when tear streams wallow into a river

then gather into an ocean of cries.

I too, must be among them.

But my tears don't flow outwards,

dripping down my face like the start of rain.

Am I a person of such shallowness

that I shan't shed my sorrow?

Am I a selfish being, unable to cry at the loss of
a loved one?

Am I an organism that only pities oneself and
seldom another?

Is it that I've been swallowed by my greed

that nothing but my own death reduces me to
tears?

Am I as such?

4

WHERE THE SHADOWS KISS THE SUN

Unspoken devotion

Without saying a word,

you told me so much.

Without any actions,

you made me feel so much.

Without sight,

you have showed me so much.

Without sound,

you have made hear so much.

Without victuals,

you have nourished me so much.

Without water,

you have quenched my thirst so much.

Without life,

you have made me live.

And yet I ask but one thing from you.

How can you love such a monster like me?

With all your heart and soul you give to me,

yet I am not able to repay it back.

The Weight of Love

You ask me, if I would die for you.

But I ask, why you want me dead.

You tell me about heroes who would let you go
to save everything.

But what about the villain who would sacrifice
everything to save you;

to be with you?

Someone who would leave the world to burn in
agony so that you can live along aside them.

Would you be proud?

Would you still love me if I were such a
person?

Would you stay by my side even if I were a
villain>

If I were to embody the one character you hate
so much,

would you still care for me?

Would you believe that the one you love — me,

the person who you expressed your undying
hatred towards

— is also me?

Dare I say, that if not then, I can no longer bear
the weight of this world.

I will sacrifice myself for you,

so as to see you live a better life with someone,

someone who you love truly and would never
ask these words;

Would you die for me?

Because darling, I have already died;

a million times over for you.

And today, might be the last.

Living death

I would not die for you — no,

that is far too easy.

I'd live for you, I'd live

if you asked me to.

Because in the end,

it's only you, me and the world

dancing with ourselves.

A forbidden love;

against the living kind,

that ours is, in which

sacrifice is all to easy.

So I'll say this again,

I won't die for you,

I will live for you.

Eternal dance

The way you make me happy, it's impeccable.

It feels as though we are inseparable.

Fated to meet by chance,

We fell deep into a trance.

A never ending saga of emotions;

Life-long opera with notions.

In which my devotion

can't be recreated, unless it's you.

As the earth is to the moon,

I will be to you soon.

Dancing with eachother till the end of time,

Or atleast until we die — but forever encased

in a book for the next rhyme.

You're my world and I want to be your moon,

so that I can spend the rest of eternity dancing
around you.

Serendipity in the Void

An infinitely voidless mind

meets a voided heart

as such, creating an individual —

one mixed in such a way that not only others

shan't understand; but itself aswell.

Then, there comes along a darkness,

so engulfed in blinding light that

nothing but itself is seen.

Deprived of beings other than thyself,

Its clashes paths with one of self

expression but not solitude.

This...creature (as self proclaimed is) is a

freak of nature. Even thyself is —

alas after crossing fates with this one,

time feels more...balanced (for a lack of a better
word)

it's as if I've caught up with my surrounding,

no longer going past at speeds too brisk.

An odd serenity washes over me,

a melancholy I had yet to feel; now looming,

almost drowning in petrichor.

The obliviousness of this being provides

a sort of serendipity, if I may. But moreover,

surfaces a complexity of emotions that

strand me in a paradox of obscurity.

Feelings dafted with perplexity with dim

my righteousness and draft me to ponder
pareidolia.

Do you doubt me, my love?

Do you doubt me, my love?

The love that I hold for you?

The same love that sparked to life

when I heard your beautiful voice?

Alas, my darling, I need your trust;

a trust in me and my devotional love.

My heart is in your hands;

my soul, my mind, my sanity,

my thoughts, my life — my entire existence

as a whole is all yours;

yours to hold, play, to use,

to control as you please.

My darling, every thought that passes

cannot by without another of you strung close.

Your voice reads every letter you send.

You've infected me, my love —

A plague I wish would last my life.

Do you still doubt me, my love?

In the Labyrinth of Time

A glimpse of you enough;

—enough to last me a lifetime.

The moment I hear your voice;

such a soothing melody — everything

comes to a standstill. My surroundings

stop in place but time rushes faster.

Every hour spent with you barely feels as such,

but rather as minutes or mere seconds.

Although, every second without you feels like
years;

stretching, never-ending, tugging at my
patience,

I sit still; while everyone moves past time.

Oh, how time plays with me and slows down;

as if, to remind me, I am just another individual

among billions in this labyrinth without you.

Eternity in Your Embrace

Though the days seem long,

and nights even longer

I still year for the eternity;

the eternity it takes to meet you.

The satisfaction of full=filled cravings.

Feather soft touches and your voice finally
undistorted

— soothing and unnerving. Embraces which
last longer than the normal bunch; as if to
convey a flood of emotions.

The rush of blood in my cheeks: as soon as I
catch

you in sight, and the , and the streams of tears
as soon as you leave.

My sweet serenity, a melancholy string of
memories,

a surprising gift to keep safe till the end of
time.

My haven of serendipity, my adoring melody,

my joy, my prized possession, my hope, my
faith,

and dare I say, my reason to continue in the
living world.

Waiting, just to cherish the moments I can

encapture and encase with you.

Nothing can compare to you. Every thought
racing

through my mind seems to be connected to
you — my love.

So, be my everything and enthrall this life with
me

and supposedly every other life we have;
together.

5

CRIMSON WHISPERS

Liminal

I'm being suffocated.

An unbreakable silence

creating a void in my eyes

All I see is darkness,

but its getting brighter,

brighter than all the stars of the night sky put
together.

It's blinding almost.

And now, all I gaze is the anti-void;

a place of pure just concentrated with
nothingness.

I close my eyes for a minutes, or two;

there is nothing.

Alas, that nothing was everything.

Waking slowly with my eyes half-shut,

laying in my room,

where I'm glad it's just another afternoon
dream.

Echoes in the Storm

The petrichor of the rain combined with

the sounds of thunder bring solace to a mind of
my own.

As I lay here, down under

A capsule of mine, set in stone.

I wait, patiently for someone to phone.

A broken soul, still healing

that's fearing

this world, hearing

night, feeling

bitter sweet and ending

the sight of ringing.

Hearing colors and seeing sounds

crimson waves and disturbing rounds

reflections of rain; drops of a mirror

parallel dimensions and wormhole craters.

The Weight of Unbelonging

You're trying to hold running water in your
hands.

But all it does is engulf your hand in a warm
embrace and flows through the cracks in your
palms.

Tell me what place am I in,

For my birth is a sin.

Both heaven and hell alike shun me to the side.

While the nigh is high,

with this ever-lasting melody,

let me drown in you;

your gaze, your voice,

and your heavy grabbing presence.

I'll engrave you into my body,

into my soul, into my brain,

and, everything that I own.

The Silent Gaze

We look up at the stars.

But do they gaze back?

They blink and glimmer many a times.

What are they facing?

It's a wonder,

How they shine so brightly

even though they burn themselves?